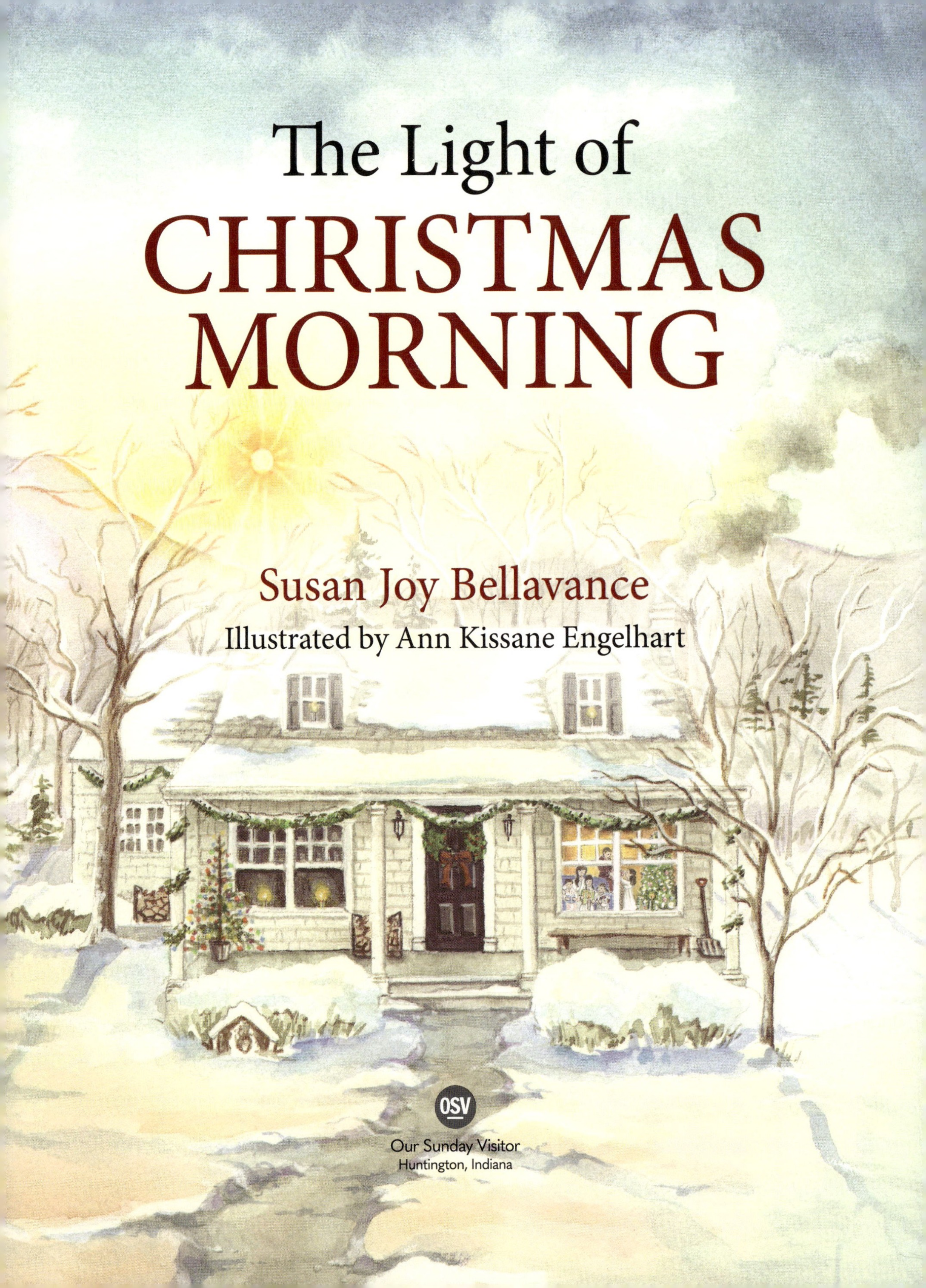

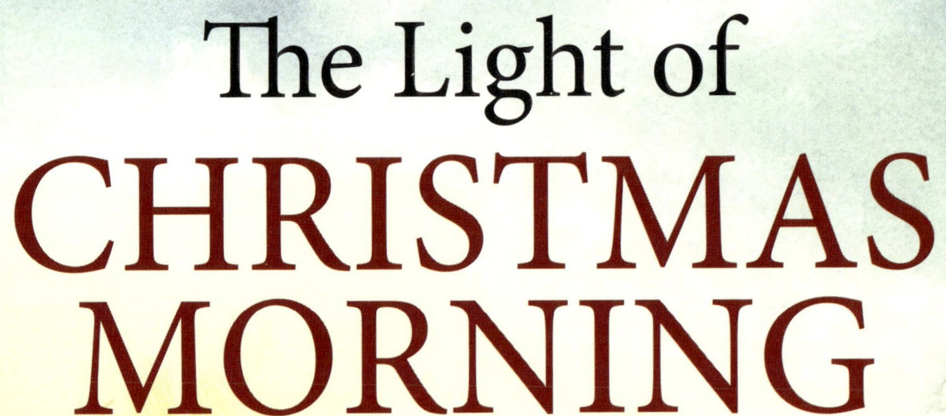

The Light of CHRISTMAS MORNING

Susan Joy Bellavance

Illustrated by Ann Kissane Engelhart

OSV

Our Sunday Visitor

Huntington, Indiana

29 28 27 26 25 2 3 4 5 6 7 8 9

Our Sunday Visitor Publishing Division
Our Sunday Visitor, Inc.
200 Noll Plaza
Huntington, IN 46750
www.osv.com
1-800-348-2440

ISBN: 978-1-68192-642-1 (Inventory No. T2511)
1. HOLIDAY—Christmas.
2. RELIGION—Holidays—Christmas & Advent.
3. RELIGION—Christianity—Catholic.
LCCN: 2021939027

Cover and Interior design: Amanda Falk
Cover art: Ann Kissane Engelhart
Interior art: Ann Kissane Engelhart and AdobeStock

PRINTED IN THE UNITED STATES OF AMERICA

Presented to

From

Date

I dedicate this book to my beloved grandchildren. I pray you will always welcome the Infant Jesus on Christmas morning and carry him to the tree with a song on your lips and joy in your heart, the way your moms did every Christmas.

"Ama Posey" (SJB)

For my brothers and sisters, Billy, Carolyn, Bob, Mary Jean, Lawrence, Katie, Tom, and Melanie, in memory of all of those wonderful Christmas mornings that we shared together in Douglaston.

Ann Kissane Engelhart

Traditions

Family traditions cradle our hearts at Christmas. They comfort us with remembrance while creating new memories. Yet Christmas is always new. With the coming of the Christ Child, God pours his grace upon the world, refreshing hearts, reviving souls, and restoring hope.

The Light of Christmas Morning shares a family tradition honoring the divine gift of the Savior who comes to us, arms wide open, desiring to be received and longing to be loved.

Perhaps it is a tradition you will want to share!

Susan Joy Bellavance

Oh, night so beautiful! Our family gathers for Mass on Christmas Eve. There are uncles, aunts, and cousins from near and far away.

The night is bright with carols and candlelight. There are grateful hearts and glowing faces. The bells ring with joy. Christ our Savior is born!

Nana and Papa's house is nearby. Everyone brings something delicious to share. Look at all the cousins! Nana and Papa are so happy to see us.

"Merry Christmas, everyone!"

There are hugs and handshakes, family stories and laughter. See the little ones run zigzag through the guests!

Sleepy, sleepy children, it's time to go home. "Merry Christmas, Nana and Papa!" we say with our kisses. Look! It's snowing! We drive along snow-lined roads to the other side of town.

Here is our little house peeking out of the woods. Blustery winds mound snowdrifts against the picket fence. Snowflakes sparkle and swirl around the porch lights, piling up to the windowsills.

Mom and Dad carry sleepy children from the car, so late, so late to bed! We spend a little time together near the twinkling Christmas tree.

It's covered with angels and stars, just like the night sky over Bethlehem long ago. There will be gifts all around it on Christmas morning.

On a low table in front of the tree is our Advent wreath. There are three purple candles and one pink. During Advent, we lit these candles every evening during our prayers.

How low they have melted. They are almost all gone! In the center of the wreath stands a lovely image of the Blessed Mother, her hands folded in prayer. Just like us, she waited a long time for Christmas Day and the coming of her sweet baby, the most precious gift.

Now we are off to bed, tucked in with a final kiss, and each bedroom door is closed.

Mom and Dad still have one more important thing to do — the most important thing of all.

From a hidden place, Mom gathers the small wooden crib filled with straw that holds the little Baby Jesus. Around his head is a golden halo. His little arms are reaching out. His face is smiling. You can feel the blessing in his eyes.

Dad tiptoes into one of the bedrooms and leaves the Precious Guest next to the bed. Ever so silently he slips away.

Someone will wake on Christmas morning to find the Baby Jesus at their bedside, just waiting to be held. Who will it be?

There is not much sleep on Christmas Eve. Long before the sun rises, everyone piles into Mom and Dad's room. Of course, we must wake them up!

"Merry Christmas, Mom and Dad!"

"I have Baby Jesus!" someone exclaims.

Mom hands everyone a candle, and Dad lights them one by one. Then Mom begins a Christmas carol, and we all join in.

We carry Baby Jesus through the house as the candles fill each room with light, and our voices fill the house with song.

Now we come to the Christmas tree. There are presents everywhere! We place Baby Jesus next to the Advent wreath, near the Blessed Mother.

We set our candles all around him as Dad leads us in prayer:

Thank you, God, Our Father, for giving us your Divine Son. Thank you, Blessed Mother, for your yes to God that brought forth Jesus, Our Savior, and for giving him to all of us.

Dear Jesus, we want you to be the King of our family, the King of our home. We ask you to always be the King of our hearts. Bless us and stay with us. You are the Light of Christmas morning!

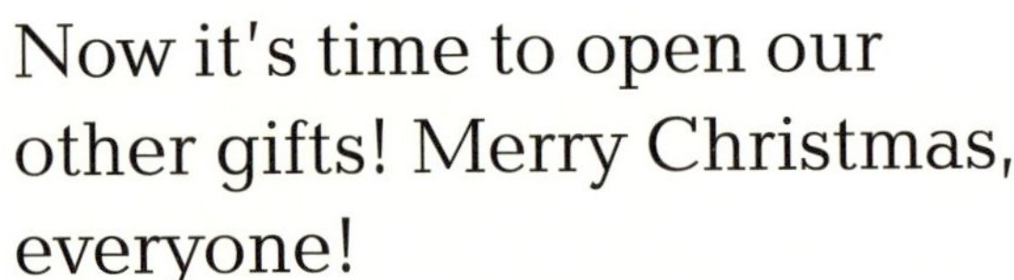

Now it's time to open our other gifts! Merry Christmas, everyone!

May the Light of Christmas
morning shine in your home, too!

ABOUT THE AUTHOR

Susan Joy Bellavance served with the Missionaries of Charity for three years, later becoming an elementary and junior high parochial schoolteacher, and a founding member of Mount Royal Academy in Sunapee, New Hampshire. She served many years as a catechist and youth formator and is currently a spiritual supporter of the Marian Missionaries of Divine Mercy. Susan's other published works are *King of the Shattered Glass* and *Will You Come to Mass?* Susan and her beloved husband, Dale, reside in metropolitan Newbury, New Hampshire. They have two daughters, Sophia and Marguerite, and two sons-in-law, Jonathan and David, and each couple has a brand-new baby.

ABOUT THE ILLUSTRATOR

Ann Kissane Engelhart is an accomplished watercolor artist, illustrator, and educator. *The Light of Christmas Morning* is her eighth illustrated book. She has worked with Amy Welborn to produce the children's books *Friendship with Jesus*, *Be Saints!*, *Bambinelli Sunday*, and *Adventures in Assisi*. She collaborated with Nancy Brown and Regina Doman on *The Chestertons and the Golden Key* and with Donna-Marie Cooper O'Boyle on *Our Lady's Message to Three Shepherd Children and the World*. Her portraits and still-life and landscape paintings are featured in galleries and private collections. Ann lives in New York with her husband and has two grown children.